María's Book

María's Book

Poems

Dave Oliphant

ALAMO BAY PRESS
SEADRIFT•AUSTIN

Copyright © 2016 by Dave Oliphant

All rights reserved. No part of this book may be reproduced in any form without permission in writing from the publisher, except by a reviewer who may quote brief passages in a review.

Cover illustration: *Tapestry of La Chimba* by María Oliphant. Malta, Illinois, 1974.

Book Design: ABP

For orders and information:
Alamo Bay Press
Pamela Booton, Director
825 W 11th Ste 114
Austin, Texas 78701
pam@alamobaypress.com
www.alamobaypress.com

Library of Congress Control Number: 2016943577
ISBN: 978-1-943306-01-5

to Darío & Elisa

Contents

- 1 María's Albums
- 3 María's Alstroemeria
- 5 María's Antiques
- 8 María's Ark
- 10 María's Bath
- 12 María's Birds
- 14 María's Birthmark
- 15 María's Butterflies
- 17 María's Clock
- 19 María's Complaint
- 20 María's Crackers
- 22 María's Cross
- 25 María's Diet
- 27 María's Dresses
- 28 María's Ears
- 30 María's Genealogy
- 34 María's Goodwill
- 36 María's Hands
- 37 María's Heart
- 39 María's Hem
- 41 María's *hermana*
- 52 María's Ideas
- 54 María's Kieffer Pears
- 56 María's Lamp
- 58 María's Larkspur
- 62 María's Maine Coon Cat
- 65 María's Mandolin
- 66 María's Mask

68	María's Meals
70	María's Memo
71	María's Memory
78	María's Menagerie
82	María's Metempsychosis
83	María's Miracles
84	María's Movies
89	María's New Mexico
93	María's Paint
95	María's Photograph
97	María's Radio
99	María's Readings
101	María's Reality
102	María's Redecoration
105	María's Saint
107	María's Set Piece
110	María's Sewing Machine
112	María's Sleep
114	María's Smile
117	María's Souvenir
119	María's Squirrels
121	María's Tambourine Man
123	María's Tapestry
125	María's Treatments
127	María's Voices
136	María's Wool
138	María's Yards
145	Acknowledgments
147	About the Photographs
149	About Dave Oliphant

María's Book

María's Albums

narrate the stories of two lives together
of children half-Texan she came to bear
from a fated union of our cultures differ
her own in Chile she left behind forever

on their pages each's disparate thought
mine in an accent like a Scottish brogue
a softer & warmer her Spanish brought
combined in binders covered with cloth

patterned prints on spines embroidered
with dates all begin & end each January
each tracing months from the same 28th
& its celebration of another anniversary

with flowers bought & books inscribed
the suppers eaten out & movies at times
in a B & B smokehouse spending a night
a gift of the kids saved quarters & dimes

memories recorded from places had lived
mostly towns & cities she'd never choose
only treasured for where a first word said
quiet or trying moments not about to lose

so determined all those she must preserve
yet complains there isn't the time it takes
for selecting the photo will better capture
the son or the daughter at each special age

the leisure needed for her writing by hand
drawing her pictures to replace those miss
stolen when the family had moved by train
a worthless box of snapshots o so priceless

the death of pet or relation the greater loss
recounting each with a photograph recalls
a dog cat or the needles would dip & cross
as Gala knitted before a final evening walk

phrases jotted down from elementary tales
Miss Foy's "I'm sick & tired" said to a class
how fit them in between the fixing of meals
doing laundry & the endless dishes to wash

with ironing awaiting after her library work
no hours left for assembling of each souvenir
of her teenage violinist in Mozart's Salzburg
her ballerina danced in the annual *Nutcracker*

her job part-time but her cooking never ends
weeding & watering of beds in need of a rain
others to make & all the mopping & dusting
darning of sox a tub & sinks scrubbing clean

yet her colorful volumes all but filling the case
scrapbooks spanning decades now nearly four
notes in an unadorned prose of a natural grace
composed in her tongue some have rated poor

though rich to any readers of her native words
those all blessed by her annals & a selflessness
in collecting sedulously both sad & humorous
crammed into the space her only closet affords

María's Alstroemeria

not knowing what gift
to buy for her
to celebrate our 48th
then found this flower

with its lance-shaped leaves
& on its flare-hued
petals dash-like upright streaks
as if sparks spewed

against their orangey-yellow skies
from the harmless volcanoes
of livid vivid ovaries
& after thinking those

with Incan or Peruvian
lilies their non-Linnaean names
to her might mean
but too-bright gaudy flames

read on the label
hybrid of summer-grown Brazilian
with the winter-bred perennial
from her own thin

land north to south
of her elongated Chile
she has lived without
for almost now half-a-century

not knowing the length
love's fire would last
while this bouquet's one-week
guarantee has already passed

yet uprooted from the
earth in a vase
of water still lovely
as she who place

of birth did sacrifice
& her relations' lives
for mine me this
match endures & thrives

María's Antiques

would need no dealer
to judge their worth
no auctioneer to call

for an opening bid
on her buck bow
saw with its symmetrical

wooden cheeks held in
tension by its rusted
turnbuckle parallel to the

length of its rusty
teeth had given next
to nothing for when

the neighbor held his
moving sale not for
lopping off branch or

limb but to hang
its wide H upon
the kitchen wall to

rest its longer handle
along the frame of
the adjacent bedroom door

for who would make
an offer on her
padlock without a key

purchased in a Chilean
store whose owner listed
on a sign the

amount of time he
would give to customers
& compadres none to

those with "bright ideas"
two hours to those
invited to lunch more

to those had come
to buy or pay
her latest from two

doors down at an
estate sale run by
the elderly lady's surviving

son carried the lawn
mower here with its
wheels no longer roll

its push handle now
leans against the backyard
fence no grass to

cut just her shrubs
her flowers in beds
& red clay pots

her collectibles rated at
less than she paid
but more to her

for materials & shapes
the lives they touched

& were needed by

for their stainless blades
or their protective steel
kept their treasures safe

valued most for just
themselves not so much
for any use they

had or yet may
serve but rather their
meaning mainly lies in

taking her back in
time to golden years
they still can lend

to her her family
& friends while best
of all her relics

keyed unlocked & lubricated
these lines for appraising
her heart & mind

María's Ark

did it come from Goodwill
or another garage sale in this
subdivision of Anderson Mill

on Public TV the panel Bill
Moyers gathered for *Genesis*
argued whether it meant

a cruel God could even kill
His own creation not of course
Noah & his motley crew

the one family on the block
who followed His rules
as when He said to

build it & Noah did
stocking it up
while the neighbors jeered

to him his God so good
that any not doing His will
was in his Middle English *wood*

but even in the surviving
Mystery play
his wife would not leap on

unless her gossips everyone
could all come too
until at last Shem their son

had to drag her aboard
with camels polecats & swine
for the forty days of manure

here the animals are flat
cut out surely on an assembly line
painted gray or brown

facing in profile all in pairs
elephants giraffes lions & sheep
& how did the latter get along

how ever did the former fit
all now seeming to move
toward these miniature steps

at rest on the fireplace mantel
up against the hull of this ship
its roofed house set in the middle

to be loaded with symbols
from that biblical tale
the dove with

its olive of peace
the rainbow sign of
an end to revenge

but just as much
the simple design
of two of each

male & female
climbing on together
knowing her this must have been

what she had in mind
when she spotted
& had to have

her bargain buy

María's Bath

    locked herself in there & left us all
    panting here outside this door
    let kids pets & hubby know
    in no uncertain terms
    was not to be disturbed

    with her beyond our sight & touch
    are feeling low & utterly lost
    stand or pace about & listen hard
    for sounds of water run or poured
    for the dead bolt shot to life

    hear it & sniff her aroma emerge
    renewed by luffa after all her chores
    soaked & sponged with lavender soap
    rinsed off & now more lovely & soft
    rubbing her again all whine & purr

    • • •

    despite the caulk applied & smoothed
    more than once from its smelly tubes
    with their guarantee the job would last
    & plastic tiles have touched up twice
    first with a yellow paint she simply hates
    & then with something called "rustoleum"
    whose label claimed it would stop the ugly stains
    or money back yet those have started again
    at the edge of the unsightly mildewed tub
    where half-submerged she stretched herself
    with her brown eyes fully closed upon
    her modest pair of lily pads
    this rent-house room now misses so
    having to fall back on its glaring fixtures
    its garish color none she would ever have

the one the landlord said to leave alone
told her rudely just to let it be
& this recalls such dreams of her
coming here with her book to read
with her apple pared to eat
to add more water hot or cold
with her little wondrous toes

& yet on revisiting the scene
it only reveals on the bathtub rim
her Chilean author's wet memoir
her bitten core
rusting with all the rest of it
no other sign
not another left behind
even the ring washed down the drain
& with the mirror now unfogged
stare vacantly at a scrawny Texan neck
instead of catching the hoped-for glimpse
just the reflection of all her loveliness
set against this dingy enamel
yet just to know she bathed in here
puts such shabbiness head & shoulders above
the most luxurious sunken brand
& turns this cheap paint job into
a pure primeval pond
viewed as through a clearing in
Creation's mist
regains this room's lost innocence
dresses it in the freshest fruit & shade
recovered as if by the pages she turned
with soft warm ungrasping fingers
the watermarked promise
of a garden plot
never to end nor would ever change

María's Birds

it isn't that the doves jays cardinals
or the mockingbirds belong to her
but the feeders & the green plastic bath
she's placed outside this patio window
bring them here whenever they please
to peck at her store-bought sunflower seeds

to dip their beaks or splash their wings
no walls of wire to keep them out or in
coming & going by their own routine
as at suppertime they always arrive
first one pink-footed dove then six or seven
flapping & maneuvering under the arbor's vines

its grape leaves shading their seeds & water
as each alights on her larger redwood roof
then hops down onto its platform holds
a box made out of cedar
heaped full with black or empty hulls
the latter if she hasn't replenished

their daily supply
their breasts too big to land or fit upon
the tiny wooden porches
of the smaller closed-in type
with its see-through panes on two
of four rectangular sides

only the chickadees or titmice
can reach the seeds drop through
an opening beneath the glass
says she'll buy a book to identify
those whose names remain unknown
though recognized by their crests

or their slightly reddish bands
as she watches at evening with such delight
while eating her vegan meal
agreeing with Lindbergh who late in life
declared if he had to choose between
the planes he flew

his famous Spirit of St. Louis
& the many models he'd flown in since
he would rather have her feathered friends
but how would she visit her people in Chile
of course the neighbors' cats prefer them too
over bags or cans of kitty food

tries shooing them away when they lie in wait
but those will come as freely as birds
leap the fence & over potted plants before they fly
leave in the shrubbery just a span of wings
more often of a taunting mocker
like the one dared dive & strut too close

or one each morning who always sang
from the mildew-resistant white crape myrtle
his varied pitches his seemingly endless tones
but those caught on coming to bathe or feed
bother her so much more
feels deeply her love had done them in

though every regret has remained outweighed
by a need to see their sudden unfathomable flight
this & their colors & their nervous twitches
sketched with kernels & the garden hose
by this artist whose special airway guests
put on in her own backyard their death-defying shows

María's Birthmark

on her upper arm the right outer
some skin stains slightly darker
a tan sea with archipelagic isles
or a planet circled by satellites

if inhabited watching never tells
yet near enough each night
on turning her way to observe
a sand-colored tumbling surf

beaches invite an exploratory kiss
from there to press her warm soft lips
cover a lower row of crooked teeth
another "fault" would ever keep

then reach to touch uneven toes
rub what to her is an outsized nose
nibble the lobes of conspicuous ears
caress closed eyes have known few tears
except when Gala Sapo or Mushto died

stroke full-bodied hair now tinted to hide
where silver is springing among brunettes
the former she'd yank out yet nothing corrects
nor needs to such "flawed" topographic features
exterior to a comely inscape her surface pictures

María's Butterflies

because they are only
passing through they won't
be staying long doesn't
know their Latin names

just recognized by their
pattern & size the
smallest of all a
pale-yellow had spotted before

swarming here from Mexico
smeared on grills &
windshields of speeding cars
unfluttering on asphalt lanes

nor can she tell
the type of bush
surely a sage with
woody stems & serrated

leaves attracts their weightless
wings more than any
brighter color stronger or
subtler scent even though

this one's flower bluer
than the one out
back with its bloom
of a lighter shade

unlike them she herself
has stayed on through
every season of unbearable
heat cedar fever &

even my exaggerated fits
when afterwards like the
orange-&-black had lit on
her I'm drawn to

settle down on finding
she offers as ever
fragrant delectable nectar as
freely as blossoms give

María's Clock

tolls of her distant past
yet as close as all
her loved ones here

though muffled after
she had it cleaned
its chime still rings

upon the hour
& at the half
to bring them back

long summer nights in Chile
in her country's "little north"
of how with supper over

Aguirre would make them sit
cousins all so dying
to hide 'n' seek outside

but would have to hear
his reading of
La Chimba's week-old news

as word by word
only now in this Texas home
do his facts & figures

all add up
kept current still
by her childhood mind

ever behind in those
happy happy days
more happy with

each pendulum swing
each tick & tock returns
the way they squirmed

in hardwood seats
their giggling together
when Gala would give her girls

a look of disapproval
she dutiful & intent on listening to
his reading of every dated notice

now hears each clear again
can see it all unchanged
as in the temporal shape

these Roman numerals take
on this brass-rimmed cracked
white porcelain face

passed over by a short & longer hand
recounting for her that timeless age
page by mystical page

María's Complaint

is not the
one 19th-century medical
men came up

with on diagnosing
women as hysterical
& weak such

physicians prescribed for
them no exercise
just rest isolation

& opium since
hers rather concerns
my being in

her clever conceit
an ivory-billed woodpecker
some contend does

not exist this
one upstairs in
his ivory tower

tapping away at
his keyboard while
downstairs she watches

television & for
the sightings few
& far between

María's Crackers

is a title only
happens to play upon
the fact she's crazy

about this orange tabby
named by the neighbor's
late New Jersey mother-in-law

whom the daughter-in-law it
seems disliked & him
too whom I have

called a Georgia crack-cocaine
from the addiction he
has caused in her

& the cost after
Blackie bit his left
front leg & it

abscessed till he couldn't
walk had to carry
him to Dr. Kim

the vet who beneath
his coat found a
chip in his skin

identified his owner as
that awful woman who—
for having rejected this

adopted ring-tailed darling pet
wakes us up in
the middle of the

night jumping onto the
bed (not to mention
the bill for surgery

antibiotics & a rabies
shot) & for not
having offered to pay

—will one day she
tells her bratty cat
surely burn in hell

María's Cross

besides at times the
one I've been for
her to bear another

is made of pine
lacquered black with straw
cut in minute diamond

shapes & appliquéd on
its horizontal & vertical
beams in patterns of

eight-point star-like flowers with
a single petal in
between & each a

quadrilateral arranged in either
fours or sixes &
balanced down or across

the humble cruciform with
its elaborate but delicate
floral design centered upon

its pair of timbers
all this the patient
work of Diana Lujan

purchased in Corrales at
the folk-art market of
Old San Ysidro Church

dates from 1868 its
cracked adobe walls shining
with yellow flecks of

summer & winter hay
harvested from simple grasses
oat barley timothy &

the wheat of gold
split sliced & glued
in a traditional Spanish

way brought back by
Eliseo Rodríguez during WPA
he a "New Mexican

Treasure" she had to
visit to see his
roods so exquisite in

rooms he built himself
already she had viewed
in Santa Fe his

life-sized tableau & too
his wife Paula's beauteous
santos but she ill

in bed while he
at 92 still happy
to show & tell

as his fan snapped
pictures & asked him
how he'd recovered his

lost religious art &
later photographed on the
plaza walk a bronze

plaque celebrates the man
whose crucifixes she all
but worships with their

stations each of straw

María's Diet

no physician she had seen
here in the capital city
of this Lone Star State

could find any reason for
the aches & pains in
her every joint arms legs

back & neck or why
when she walked her feet
went snap crackle & pop

ran every kind of test
sent her to a physical
therapist declared her muscles limp

tried to "pump them up"
but neither exercises nor lifting
weights nothing would bring relief

not until she traveled to
her native land & saw
Dr. Silva a Chilean who

by peering into her iris
& glimpsing signs no x-rays
ever reveal diagnosed her fibromyalgia

his practice not limited to
traditional cures but including hot
wet towels cold mud packs

herbal teas but most of
all her vegan meals no
meat milk eggs or cheese

her friends asking her how
can anyone live like that
on salad fruit & veggies

in reply would tell them
long ago Thoreau her hero
wrote cows survive on grass

but if she herself cannot
neither can she taste again
eggplant baked with olive oil

or Irish potatoes wrapped in
foil since the two contain
solanine can cause arthritic pain

debilitates by infecting connective tissue
yet now she's doing fine
thanks to food she never

consumes & to her countryman
spied & identified symptomatic motes
with his beamless medical eye

María's Dresses

no matter their prices or how they've looked
found hanging on dismal bargain-store racks
stacked for sale in a stranger's garage or yard
in the end all alike have been transformed

not alone by laundering & changing a hem
by adding a bow or redoing a gaudy collar
by letting the waist out or by taking it in
but by covering clinging & softly conforming

like the simple white of our wedding day
made from her own design by her Tía Pepa
only showed her bare tanned arms between
her short sleeves & gloves of cotton netting

silk organdy to the throat & down to the floor
trimmed with a velvet sash of peaches pink
laced ruffle over tips of delicate slippered feet
a ribbon held her hair & the eagerly lifted veil

María's Ears

    are a little
    larger than some
    & will if

    they care to
    listen better than
    most & through

    them can whistle
    any pop-song tune
    or movie theme

    even whole sections
    of symphonies they
    once have heard

    at night removes
    her earrings from
    lobes pierced at

    birth & propped
    up by her
    pillows begins to

    read when then
    I hum &
    um-yum-yum on nibbling

    upon soft &
    delicious tips the
    only bedtime sounds

    am permitted to
    make since these
    cannot compete with

her concentrating on
another writer's words
whisk her away

to where to
such caresses they're
both stone deaf

María's Genealogy

a lapsed Catholic herself
somewhat like her mother
who never went to mass
but ever offered a prayer

yet if unanswered right away
quickly appealed to another saint
though at least her younger daughter
has attended on the two big dates

his winter birth & springtime death
though instead of the Roman church
has kidded perhaps she may convert
to the polygamous Latter-Day faith

smiles to remember in Chile
how all along her Pyramid Street
neighbors would yell in warning
then close their shutters & doors

at the coming of an identical
white-shirted necktied pair
though always one short one tall
appearing each year to explain

in broken Spanish the origins of
their sacred *Book of Mormon*
though saddened now to recall
a young man murdered in Austin

who had served his time by walking
each unfriendly belligerent block
to bring the news to every race
others sent farther for photographs

of the records of married & deceased
in every out of the way diocese
Ovalle where on January 12th of '44
Gala was delivered of my pride & joy

her second girl child who prefers
dusty La Chimba to anywhere else
another unheard-of country place
her grandfather's in the little north

needed to know of its former life
ways her mother had had to go
which train she took to school
in the southern town of Rengo

wanted as well to identify
those her line descended from
& to find them had to drive
to their Family History Center

to order from Salt Lake City
handwritten archives on microfilm
to view in Texas the Chilean names
to decipher five centuries of entries

for reconstructing her Aguirre tree
all the wedded cousins & their issue
the generations on her maternal side
down to her own & her sister's too

tracing back to 1540 when out of Perú
Francisco most loyal captain to Valdivia
crossed with that conqueror the Atacama
second worst desert in all the world

born 1500 in Talavera de la Reina
he her first relation in Chile
governor-defender of La Serena
defeated Drake & his buccaneers

had marauded her native coast
burning homes & inventories
accurately kept for every parish
her forebears born & buried

Paco later mayor of Santiago
capital city where she came to accept
for this gave up her storied nation
here where she's read how at sixty-nine

he lay imprisoned in La Plata
awaiting three years for delayed release
by order of the King would hear & respond
to news they had dragged his faithful servant

before the Inquisition in Chuquisaca
marched in chains from Tucumán
back across the Andes & the Atacama
to be accused of heresy in word & deed

ninety crimes against religion
among them how not hearing mass
could bring no harm to those he believed
commend in hearts their souls to God

how Plato could equal in thought
the Gospel according to the Evangel John
how excommunication frightened little men
not him who never feared dishonest priests

would eat not fish but meat on Fridays
on holidays had his Indians work the fields
declared heaven & earth could pass away
but not the truth he was pledged to say

then bareheaded forced to confess his errors
by bishop & viceroy had grown to covet
the authority vested in him by Philip II
those at last had convinced the throne

the Americas needed to sit a Tribunal
whose accusations continued till '76
when he returned to his fruits & flowers
orchards & gardens won in Araucanian wars

at 81 after 40 years & just before the end
writing from New Spain his final lines
declared he had faithfully served his sovereign
along with chattel household & offspring

spending 300 thousand of his personal pesos
losing brother sons son-in-law & grandsons
in discovering subduing & settling a kingdom
in the name of his highness whose hands & feet

his vassal kissed from the blue Pacific
of her long thin land she now revisits
by virtue of that conquistador's words
& those who trust in the power of prayer

to save them from eternal death
& every ancestor who ever lived
before that sacred revelation
of their founder Joseph Smith

María's Goodwill

used donations prices lower
policy of hiring handicapped
these brought her here
for plates to catch

water from potted indoor
plants as I listen
in this sun-warmed car
to the classical station

its early music ballad
after a *Decameron* tale
of Abbess who had
gotten caught with wimple

not hers as knock
at door would discover
her dishabille her shock
at underwear of lover

then noticing the store
name across its sign
repeated over & over
in one continuous line

I shuffle the letters
of the words combined
& find thirty others
form questions & rhymes:

will good do ill
low gold glow idol
old wid woo lil
wool wig gild doll

dill log lid wold
wood oil gill goo
owl god go wild
igloo dog dig loo

if Boccaccio in translation
has word order changed
is the language newfangled
or still but secondhand

such concerns of course
were none of hers
who had in mind
watering flowers in wintertime

yet whatever she's needed
has nourished poetry's leaves
fed roots & seeded
singing's parts of speech

María's Hands

her own are nothing like the ones
in El Greco's ecclesiastical portrait
of a Cardinal in cape red cap & lace
rendered with thin elongated fingers
be-ringed & extended on elegant cloth
hers though short not stubby at all
of a feminine form yet softly strong
her delicate nails with quarter moons
never changeable from full to a sliver
uncovered with polish or silver glitter
whether peeling beets carrots or onions
washing pots pans lettuce or toilet bowl
the same whatever they handle or lift
pencils or pens copybooks or spirits
on her right the second digit is bent
from getting caught in a bicycle chain
a permanent mark on its larger joint
her pinky bearing a sympathetic bend
tender at times from her fibromyalgia
on the left her simple wedding band
an unadorned gold from a Chilean store
her best friend no sparkling diamond
at another shop on the Square of Arms
had the accepted name engraved inside
only once taken off as her protest sign
when found its mate removed from pain
caused by a golf club swung with it on
at school never took any typing lesson
yet her indices do as much as any two can
on any keyboard ever so accurate & quick
with gloves on has dug in the hardest dirt
in walking or sitting feel deep comfort from
holding them bare but if too sore from chores
just to have them laid on will minister & heal

María's Heart

    (or whichever organ it is
    hurts from what we miss)
    bears the tiniest tear
    in the shape of where
    she was born to be
    in her long thin native Chile
    given up against her will
    once love had made her feel
    through affection's forceful sway
    she had to forsake it & come away
    to this foreign place as any African slave
    or more like the poor & oppressed still brave
    immigrant hardship as did the Irish & Russian Jews
    for those of their own volition could choose
    to take the risk & make the voyage
    in a cramped unhealthful steerage
    if surviving to land on Ellis Island
    arriving barely to understand
    the official exam would undergo
    if answered wrong stamped mentally slow
    deported alone separated from parents whose family name
    anglicized by authorities & on Galveston Isle the same
    quarantined & lined up all in the nude
    for delousing by inspectors whose forebears earlier sued
    to enter the Redman's space any indignity ready to endure
    since each & every self so wonderfully sure
    in its innocent soul (or whatever it is
    suffers pain for future bliss)
    it would soon find freedom's hope fulfilled
    but with her longing for home unstilled
    the rip from that rift now throbs again
    its wound still seeping deep within
    & all because her coming here
    cut her off from a relationship first & forever dear
    her maiden name replaced by mine

a Scottish on paperwork she has had to sign
on her alien card rude agents review with every trip
since she'll not surrender her Chilean citizenship
& how does it make me feel
her having come against her will
o torn in two though in the end
know she's stayed & as yet no law has passed to send
her back & so have tried to believe it's right
in the Logic-versus-Emotion title fight
the decision should go to the breakable heart
(if that's the body's irrational loving part)

María's Hem

before my barefoot contessa
will baste by hand & sew
she has me measure all around

from bottom of skirt to table top
where her seductive feet
now slowly turn

to this pinning marks
the proper length
as I kneel before this table

like the pedestal I have ever
placed her on
though to her it's just

pure sacrilege
can hear her say
they're made of clay

& yet love needles
until once more
impiety sings

her inch by
inch another
fitting hymn

María's hermana

    known as Cony
    from her rabbit-like
    two front teeth

    against them she
    pushes an index
    finger as she

    muses & makes
    connections though once
    called Sapita by

    a man who
    so resented her
    staring at him

    from her toad-like
    habit of eavesdropping
    on others' talk

    observant & quite
    discerning in every
    way her taste

    ever so discriminating
    her home cozy
    from her decorations

    her own creations
    she frames herself
    one artist friend

    declaring after years
    of classroom training
    lessons in sketching

sculpting & painting
self-taught Cony can
do it all

a natural who
takes a material
selects a shade

designs & shapes
cuts or brushes
tints or collages

depicts as a
gift some native
motif on hope

chest or desk
inks blossoms of
fuchsia magellanica from

Chile's southern tip
with its deep-red
pistil its stamen

anther & filament
as precisely as
a botanist would

in her hands
rejected remnants rendered
more than they

seemed to be
she a college
dropout all but

finished her degree
in English-as-a-second-language &
would have taught

in public schools
as Gala had
for 30 years

yet Cony painfully
shy preferred to
housekeep & cook

while their mother
prepared her classes
marked the endless

papers & María
rode crushed in
a bus taken

to her library
work stamping &
repairing the battered

books arriving home
to spotless floors
clean linen delicious

meals the warmth
of walls with
fresh seasonal décor

soothing tones for
spring & summer
in winter vivid

in autumn subdued
& although grateful
Gala & María

had opposed her
having quit &
disagreed with her

when it came
to the father
Cony alone adored

for both had
learned long before
he had been

untrue & when
he went to
Rio to receive

a Brazilian prize
for another of
his cover designs

María would write
to him We're
happier here without

you Please do
not come back
Talent is no

excuse for such
abuse this at
just thirteen her

convincing words poor
Cony could never
forgive had kept

her daddy away
never to see
him ever again

dead of cancer
at last report
his radio show

his party jokes
his award-winning story
printed by a

leading press &
even María conceding
his sense of

humor his brilliant
artistic flair Cony
has from him

María taking more
after their level-headed
practical mother retained

in any fix
a happy disposition
while Cony by

turns a delight
or dynamite just
like their mercurial

dad who summed
up a friend
or foe with

a bon mot
would perfectly fit
made clever fun

of one &
all though he
himself unable to

bear mockery in
a public way
yet Cony's comic

touch reserved alone
for family at
home her witty

questions written on
paper slips to
be answered by

those whose every
peculiar trait she
knows so well

her barbed queries
can even to
their targets bring

tears of laughter
& when her
sons & daughter

fill the house
with their schoolmates
up late with

studies all are
at ease with
their adopted aunt

& confide in
her who invites
them to spend

the night feeds
& fixes them
each a pallet

while her Palestinian
spouse will foot
the bill he

whose blood seems
as thick in
her as in

their own offspring
whose feelings flow
counter to those

María holds for
Edith & Gerard
dear old friends

saved from the
Holocaust by his
having in Spain

obtained a position
the couple married
a year then

apart for ten
separated by the
Civil War reunited

in the U.S.A.
to visit Chile
in '64 he

a NASA scientist
had heard Albert
Einstein lecture &

said hardly understood
a single word
yet in German

Gerard could still
recite from Goethe
write perfect Spanish

his wife reading
far & wide
meeting María at

the binational center
& checking out
from her an

eclectic selection of
titles & then
chatting together &

afterwards the three
hiking the Andes
her childless pair

become to her
like second parents
while Cony to

find it wrong
for María to
waste her time

with such elders
instead of dating
those her age

reminding her how
at 22 she
needed to be

finding a man
differed on this
as too on

the touchy issue
of Arab &
Jew but knowing

well each other's
view they would
let it alone

María instead to
recall how she
hated having to

wear her sister's
hand-me-downs her school
uniforms stained with

ink skirts green
with avocado or
yellow with mush

from quince mashed
against sidewalk or
wall & although

unalike forever close
while the partial
Texas observer tried

his best to
take no side
yet couldn't help

but of the
two identify with
the younger more

even if felt
blest by the
welcome given by

this sister-in-law to-be
extended in spite
of her knowing

how his courting
might mean a
continent in between

with letters eagerly
awaited or the
phone to ring

María's Ideas

    at first accepted few or none
    almost all rejected out of hand
    & automatic would prefer my own

    argued hers were too much trouble
    would require money we didn't have
    though really just my giving in

    for always it was utterly clear
    hers better & made more sense
    like the faithful used VW van

    she conceived we ought to buy
    for its side door easily slides
    two seats for kids & pets

    with one removed for hauling sand
    gravel & her organic garden soil
    to transport the tiles to replace

    the dusty dirty carpets she felt
    so harmful to all our health
    & having learned the hard way

    marriage math means a little expense
    can make for a contented wife
    I had paid the asking price

    & then one day she thought
    we needed a bit more space
    yet liked no house she saw

    so decided to add to this
    & had me call for estimates
    to expand out behind the back

the first seemed way too high
so had me phone another place
Erik arriving to hear her plan

for an addition above the garage
& leaning against his pickup truck
he quickly sketched a simple design

a room for each of us
a half bath convenient to both
hers for tables & sewing machine

mine for shelves CDs & books
into hers would move a bed
on visits from family & friends

& although Erik's bid the same
his job finished right on time
& still we're taking pleasure in

this plot too saccharine for some
one true as a tragic play's
but hers with genial comic outcome

María's Kieffer Pears

    hard & huge & half-hidden
    among the thick green leaves
    of smooth-skinned gray-brown limbs
    shoot from a trunk tall as the roof

    reached by a trick she's taught
    of a ten-foot-by-four-inch board
    eaten at the edge from being before
    stuck on its side & propped by stones

    for keeping the earth in her salvia bed
    tied to either end a rusted can
    twisted & turned to snap the stems
    & hear them drop with a gentle clunk

    then ease them down & lift them out
    as mosquitoes swarm at shoes & cuffs
    with fruit already fallen from wind & rain
    drawing bees by a rich fragrant ferment

    placed on a dish in the dining room
    they call for an artist's oil & brush
    to catch their glow of reddish-pink
    freckled blush against yellow-green

    on top their stiff umbilical cords
    over smaller & larger graceful swells
    together shaped to a sensuous pair
    though for most the meat's too tough

    unsold in stores not worth the trouble
    more often than not are left to rot
    or stuffed under a Depression mattress
    softened somewhat as the indigent slept

will peal & slice & dig out knots
till blisters form on her fingertips
then simmers with sugar & cinnamon
their white flesh to a burnished tan

from the steam every room redolent
with their clean & wholesome smell
afterwards cooled & served as dessert
shared with friends know how to tell

the taste & tenderness her stewing gave
her recipe began with backyard grown
the brightness of their earliest blooms
filled her tree with a flowering of light

survived the last cold snap of spring
then cast below its snow-white shadow
gone from where each globe stayed on
to balloon full & firm the summer long

pecked at by flights of passing birds
until the time for bringing them down
to hand them over to her loving touch
works such wonders with fire & water

María's Lamp

we desperately needed one
to see to eat her suppers by
the borrowed house left un-
furnished we couldn't buy

an expensive type ready-made
beds more pressing she decided
we should purchase just a shade
for its base would use a purified-

water bottle & I *I* should
fix it all!   with her confidence
driving me on I did what I could
but cut wires short & rents

in everything my temper
touched swore I couldn't do it
tore outside to whimper
wanting so to be a poet

not a stupid handyman
came back without a poem
but loving her a better plan
for how to illumine our home

rewired refitted & taped
to her green transparent glass
(as if some verse I'd shaped)
a fixture made of brass

then tightening the socket saw
as pliers were catching hold
a gripping image of how to draw
& fasten such paradox as old

as nighttime plainer than day
& as the bulb cast clarity off the ceil-
ing paint watched it on the table lay
a cloth of light for her evening meal

María's Larkspur

a variety called
Cloudy Skies who
knows why when

its bloom's no
fluffy cumulus but
a spurred calyx

of pink violet
blue or white
prefers rich well-drained

soil ample water
will not the
catalog ads declare

rain on your
day but does
dislike to be

transplanted & looks
best in patches
clustered together although

unseen now in
the backyard where
she set them

out & yet
from there a
gully-washer swept their

seeds away &
ending up in
front between sidewalk

& curb they
rooted in dirt
under pea-sized gravel

her *Delphinium consolida*
a genus complex
as orchids although

absent any genetic
barrier to intercrossing
& in hybridizing

brings such comfort
as when this
month after the

deep winter freeze
had done in
her white dewdrop

duranta whose blossoms
draw butterfly bee
& hummingbird these

lifted their sepals
stamens styles anthers
pedicels & pistils

& for decades
the description says
will yield a

steady petal supply
& not for
her eyes alone

since just last
week two young
girls white &

black knelt on
this asphalt street
the latter snapping

a photograph for
lack perhaps of
beauty at home

carried their picture
to share it
with those may

have needed the
sight even more
if only as

a Kodacolor &
though the real
thing brown &

wither will yet
return with spring
& while too

my flower who
sowed them first
must fade as

any blossom her
stigmas left behind
will on another

day in receiving
pollen germinate her
bright consoling clouds

María's Maine Coon Cat

after his whiskered face
tufted cheeks striped legs
& perfectly rounded paws

appeared sitting upon
her backyard cedar bench
his huge yellow eyes

staring in hope & fear
she yearned to know
the life he lived before

then invented for him
an abusive history
of being left outside

in thunder & lightning
can lower him still
just as the sight of a

broom or stranger
will flatten his fluffy tail
make him growl &

run for cover under
dresser couch or bed
had arrived unsexed & bedraggled

& against every objection
her Siamese had been
trouble enough

she coaxed him in
to her home & heart
both taken over by

his long sharp claws
ruined the new front door
& though her skin unmarked

will kill her instead
with golden belly spread
protected along the windowsill

by crape myrtle photinia
abelia & bridal wreath
& thrills her when

the primal beast shows through
as he stalks among her
rosemary Mexican oregano

salvia & mint leave his mottled
coat matted & scented with
spent blooms her brushing removes

as she pets & kisses
& whispers in his ear
he's her sweetie pie

the most beautiful creature
in the whole wide world
who made it miraculously

from New England here
her unlooked-for gift
has brought such treasure

as no lottery she says
no fame or glory
could ever give

& it goes as well for her
who accepted my awkward
invitation to that

date will never forget
since as lucky as he
with his hope & fear

I too with mine
was not turned down
but let in to all of this

María's Mandolin

rests inside its orange-lined case
with its hollow form unembraced
its neck not held nor danced upon
its strings untuned & uncaressed
lifting no song nor lilting a phrase

nor can it leave the closet yet
stored beneath the sheets & spreads
the quilts & blankets for another year
shut away with children's winter wear
from before they were grown & gone

no time she says no time to play
must sweep & wash & bake & sew
how can I hope to practice now
come home you want your supper on
cook or concertize I can't do both

& so I listen to Prokofiev
his score of Romeo & his Juliet
with its contradanse for mandolins
longing to hear her fingers & lingering upon
each note they'll give upon that day

when her chords will return the tones
of her mamita's Chilean voice
can make no sound upon its own
must await for María to set it free
from death's closet & leather case

though shelved beyond her reach
can feel it ringing even now in me
its tremolos recounting every night
she's held this head & kissed the frets
till her music's filled all my emptiness

María's Mask

each night she slips
its white elastic band
over her head &

around her now gray
hair with in its
blue-green satin finish no

slits for eyes not
to masquerade not to
hide & go unrecognized

but to keep from
being awakened through curtain
or blind by the

peeping moon streetlight or
my too-bright Texas sun
for when she is

she can't fall back
asleep & must read
or arise & begin

her chores even at
four a.m. although has
yet to come to

earplugs against my snores
when I roll over
onto my back or

turn to her side
to blow like a
breaching whale disrupts her

beauty rest her dreams
I'll never sound her
deepest self have never

known can only spy
her lovely lips release
her Chilean tones whistled

Beethoven or Dylan tunes
or early music for
Arabian oud & once

removed the eyes it
reveals ever steal &
harpoon this heart again

María's Meals

ill in Chile
were yet to wed
she telephoned by
the landlady said

was deathly afraid
whatever I had
would surely spread
had other boarders

to think of too & so
she fetched me in a cab
hurried me to her home
got me into her bed

so sick it seemed
the most natural thing
being tucked between
her clean white sheets

brought a steaming bowl
of consomé
noodles boiled & served
with oil & salt

stewed apples
manzanilla tea
made whole again
by the nourishment of

her dishes prepared
day after day
have kept up strength
forever since

or was it sleeping
where Beauty had slept
on her pillow where
she had laid her head

cured most by being
so close could savor
the delicacy of
all her care

María's Memo

    made the administrators pee in their pants
    sent them scurrying to find that Chapter 9
    with the very section paragraph & line
    forbid lobbying legislators on university time

    & while we mice-men kept our profiles low
    weathering the controversy well out of sight
    she carried it to those high-ups of might makes right
    waging for all classified staff the glorious losing fight

María's Memory

her short-term is not
what once it was
though it's still long
on the distant past

what happened this morning
or just last night
or the day before
it may not recall

but from childhood in
rainy Temuco it retains
Lautaro the street named
for Ercilla's Araucanian chief

on it too Pablo
Neruda lived & also
saw *La Bota roja*
its shoemaker's red-boot sign

from summer vacations spent
in La Chimba with her
Aguirre kin she remembers
avocado & walnut trees

& still quotes the
Jonathan Winters lines of
wife returned merchandise sold
to her "milk-toast" mate

"Hello STORE it's ME!"
pinning the salesman down
& forcing him to
repeat "Customer's always right"

nor forgets politically incorrect
Seinfeld sitcom scenes of
parking in handicapped space
stealing senior's babka cake

always remind her of
all the dumb things
I've said or done
the letter published led

to a Federal case
unwise decisions acted upon
before had checked with
her but good times

too as when after
25 years vows renewed
to love & cherish
in sickness & health

María's Menagerie

one by one her brood has appeared
her Bremen animal band
until its invasion

has almost overwhelmed
only the donkey
has yet to arrive

with his pitiful song
his bray at sunset
his heehaw at dawn

she still impatient
for the smell of his sweat
his fresh green cakes

from mash or hay
while those already here
came frisky & young

unlike the bunch
in the Grimm brothers' tale
whose useful days

had come to an end
their owners bent
on drowning cooking doing them in

would make a meal
of those had served
cut back on costs of keeping them fed

of her own only
the layers have
paid their way

while she had to have
the Siamese cat declawed
to save the upholstery on the sofa bed

yet surgery came too late
for in a scampering & jumping fit
it dug a scratch

in her antique dresser
& her hand still bears a scar
from her treacherous adorable pet

the one on her wrist above her thumb
from when on wanting down
it had growled against

another lipstick kiss on its forehead fur
but has never forgotten & still regrets
the pain she made her kitten feel

with its taped bloody paws
wrapped like a challenger's fists
just before some title match

for days till the drug wore off
her Mushto looking punchy
with groggy eyes & feinting moves

her dog an ugly worthless mutt
overweight & with legs too short
too dumb to bark at would-be thieves

good for nothing but fleas
lying on flowers she nursed along
sucking the eggs of her exotic hen

Guacolda with her big green feet
lays shells of a matching tint
a cross between a Spanish breed

& a Chilean fowl
as Araucanian as her namesake in
Ercilla's epic poem

Lautaro's beloved spouse
whose dream
of his tragic death

at the hands of troops
Villagrán would lead
came true

as almost in
the Chaucer tale
his Chauntecleer's

like him her rooster a mock heroic
cocky in his spurs & crenellated comb
let the whole block know how he was here

with a morning crow nearly woke the dead
so irritated one guy two houses down
he threw bottles & stones at first

but then from his own backyard
before the kids were off to school
aimed a pump or pellet gun

at his puffed & colorful breast
took the wind right out of him
finished forever his wing-dipping dance

raccoon & possum sneaking in
to snack on her other hens
Dottie & La salvaje

after which Guacolda
before the sun had set
would cluck outside the door

fly up & peck
at the kitchen window
no more chicken coop for her

from then on would roost in the den
& was welcomed in as if this home
were Ma Kettle's in *The Egg and I*

recalls how Gala would always swear
with too much love for the animal kingdom
there's little left for humankind

it's mostly just that all are jealous
husband son & daughter of affection showered
on any brute from mongrel to her nasty cat

yet know she still has more than enough
to spread around deserved or not
though none for toads snakes or a certain neighbor

María's Metempsychosis

not to hear the rude remarks she so resents
be spared those in-laws must always hint
how awfully wrong she has raised her kids
says next time around will marry an orphan

even better will return in an animal's skin
of dog or cat eats & sleeps for half the day
barks or scratches at the door to be let in
to shrieks of delight petted watered & fed

in dishes will never wash dry nor ever fill
yet most gives pause when simply declares
will come back male be done once & for all
with lumps in the breast & a fibrous uterus

& that will leave me but a choice between
being a gay or female & how will that feel
whatever shape shade or gender she takes
paired with her again will be nirvana still

María's Miracles

    she performs them day & night
    as when she gives the cat a kiss
    on its furry blue-point face
    then lets it stretch & softly knead

    with paws against her Chilean cheek
    when husband & kids hoot & hiss
    yet believe in such a miraculous sight
    permitted even the unworthy witness

María's Movies

are none she's made herself
only those she has seen
again & again her all-time

favorite *Master & Commander* with
Russell Crowe even though she's
so opposed to violence in

life & film but can
allow it on the screen
if acting writing & cinematography

all come together as when
from his crew's cello-playing naturalist-physician
that Aussie actor learns of

an insect camouflaged as stick
or twig & disguises their
outmanned vessel as a blubber-smoking

whaler takes by complete surprise
the superior Napoleonic warship &
high too on her list

actor-director Warren Beatty as Jack
Reed in *Reds* with Diane
Keaton as Louise Bryant asks

as what would she go
with him to NYC his
wife or concubine his reply

with Thanksgiving near why not
come as a turkey Jack
Nicholson as the cynical playwright

Gene O'Neill & Henry Miller
historical witness to Communist dreams
observing with one eye closed

as much fucking went on
then as now but today
it's perverse while those showed

a bit of heart &
even love & she also
gets a kick out of

John Cusack in *High Fidelity*
with its top-ten pop-song themes
Jack Black as the record-store

clerk dresses a customer down
for his collection doesn't include
Bob Dylan's *Blonde on Blonde*

& of course Marisa Tomei
as an out-of-work hairdresser whose
biological clock's ticking away while

Joe Pesci her lawyer-fiancé knows
no courtroom procedure together in
My Cousin Vinny whose witty

script with its details like
mud in tires & cooking
grits seem only meant for

laughs but return as significant
facts & win the case
for two students wrongly accused

yet mostly she prefers to
the Hollywood epic or comic
routine such foreign-made features as

The Syrian Bride who's stopped
at the border crossing &
kept from joining her unknown

groom by the Israelis &
her own Islamic guards &
were she to leave would

not be permitted ever again
to return to her country
& this my Chilean understands

from having given up her
native land for this marriage
could have gone wrong being

resented by her countrymen from
marrying a gringo & agreeing
to go abroad with him

& suspicious here from never
becoming a citizen but ever
remaining year-after-year a registered alien

& in *The Weeping Camel*
identifies deeply with its ceremony
performed in the Mongolian Gobi

for the mother after her
difficult birth will not feed
her own white colt until

with two-stringed horse-head fiddle the
musician sings hoos hoos hoos
pleading with notes & words

for her to accept her
hungry offspring cries each morning
to suckle her nourishing milk

& adores *The Vertical Ray
of the Sun* with its
three Vietnamese daughters prepare their

parents' memorial banquet while each
in her way unhappy &
yet all beautifully affectively shot

one with a husband with
writer's block another whose spouse
visits his lover in his

other house the unwed youngest
living with her brother &
fantasizing she carries a child

or those like the Israeli
Lemon Tree pictures the injustice
of their Supreme Court ruling

against the Palestinian's grove on
upholding its being bulldozed down
& *Bliss* the gripping Turkish

flick of the innocent girl
secretly raped by the village
leader demands an honor killing

sends his son to pull
the trigger or force her
into a suicide leap but

fallen in love with her
he comes to hide her
till the truth will out

& the lives in *Cave*
of the Yellow Dog &
The Scent of Green Papaya

most of all in *Once*
with its music & love
sung & playacted from life

by Glen Hansard the Irish
singer & Markéta Irglová his
gorgeous Czech immigrant friend these

half-fictions real to her not
TV reality shows but more
like documentaries on rented DVDs

María's New Mexico

ever begins at the end
of the Santa Fe Trail
where trappers settlers & traders

after their thousand-mile overland trek
cheered & tossed their bonnets
beaver caps & broad-brimmed hats

high in the autumn air
on looking down at last
from the Sangre de Cristo's

snow-mantled peaks & glimpsing sight
of cottonwoods & aspens below
with leaves richer than even

Cíbola's gold their yellows Gustave
Baumann later engraved & other
artists minted in modernist oils

the Plaza where native craftsmen
display their rings & necklaces
silver & turquoise with squash-blossom

& bear-claw tabs mosaic inlay
pendants spread out on cloths
along the Governor's Palace walls

across from the sidewalk plaques
honor Georgia O'Keeffe Eliseo Rodríguez
Willa Cather Oliver La Farge

yet unlike the weary &
relieved she stops here only
briefly before she continues north

on the high road to
Chimayó Truchas Trampas & Peñasco
but Taos most of all

by that scenic route with
its poverty & collapsing homes
next to pricey galleries' art

or will take the Rio
Grande drive to Embudo &
Velarde by apple orchards at

Dixon past Stanley Crawford's garlic
farm with roadside stands offer
red chile ristras & in

spring rafters running rapids although
she never comes for sports
just heads for Mabel's home

& Couse's too to walk
again the former's grounds to
observe their surrounding trees &

the dovecote pigeons circle around
on gray-white wings to take
in against the clear blue

sky the sacred mountain Mabel
viewed from her upstairs room
for years has wished to

see inside where Brett &
the prudish Lorenzo painted the
bathroom window or on oppressive

summer days where Mabel drank
her lemonade the cozy winter
fireplace where she awaited return

of her wise & regal
Tony & comes to watch
the acequia ripple beneath a

footbridge near the hand-carved gate
saved from the Ranchos church
after the French archbishop unhinged

& removed its rustic doors
replaced them in the town's
now most illustrious tourist attraction

its sight etched painted &
photographed so many times from
not the front but the

bare backside's curved adobe slope
& must explore every nook
& cranny in the studio

where Couse would work upon
his fireside scenes with his
models either of Pueblo brothers

as if his own his
homage paid to their dignified
race & she's enamored too

of hand-cut beams & of
stone-filtered water she savors still
from Chilean summers recovered here

in this Indian-Hispanic-Anglo state with
its past to which she
feels akin since its Chama

& chamisa return her to
her youthful days in La
Chimba's dry & fruitful land

whose longed-for time & place
she visits again if only
through a museum exhibit case

María's Paint

after the novel by W.D. Howells

its label claims one easy coat's enough
to do the job as deodorant & patriotism
she calls the great American cover-ups
hide sweaty odor & a multitude of sins

but first she insists I will have to clean
with bleach & remove the grime before
I apply the light & darker green
picked from samples the hardware store

gave her free of charge she like Lapham's
wife determined to have the colors
changed on all the outside walls & trim
tired of seeing on windows & doors

the same ugly grayish brown so common
here in Texas where that protagonist came
then returned to rise & fall in his own
Vermont where Pert whose dearest name

he gave to his line of fancy shades
goaded Silas until he set a date & got
it done while week-after-week I've just delayed
the inevitable by resisting in cold or hot

as the brand she bought or the one
he sold from a rotten-tree mine his father
had lucked upon as I still put off the bother
of masking tape of loading the caulking gun

of climbing a ladder unreaches to gable tops
with enamel dropping in dribs & drips
on bifocals shirt pants sandals & sox

& of washing rollers brushes & stirring sticks

even as she assures me once I finish
I'll feel so virtuous & will love the fresher
look & this is true though any real pleasure
will only come from giving her her wish

María's Photograph

stranded on that proverbial desert isle
if not allowed herself
the choice would be her photograph
not one from the album stored in me
but any of the few untorn in two
& tossed away o how she hates them all!

just as much as I so cherish each
like this color print I am gazing upon
has kept her with her hair cut short
though in the beach wind blown enough
to allow far inland for this summoning up
of her breathing deeply of its salty air

with behind her head the water blue
the sky of lighter & darker shades
white splashes of clouds to either side
& she between them like a mermaid
yet it's never a fable whenever she's near
though even then it seems unreal

having her close night after night
or even to hold her years away
in this simple sleeveless top
with throat & shoulders bare
in October there at Corpus
whose Gulf coast can't compare

with Chile's brilliant stretch of sea
where a week before our wedding day
her skin took on such a radiant tan
after she'd gone with Gala & was left to mope
grew almost weak with wanting her
never guessed she'd return lovelier yet

& while there's little here to recommend
with these lukewarm waves just lazing in
crumbling sand castles too harsh to touch
even so this Texas beach still holds her in
its most becoming light
has done its best to measure up

as if somehow it knew
it must compete
was up against her vast Pacific
whose tides take in such climates
reach to distant cultures' continents
these poor shores can only dream

can hardly hope to fathom
her Arabic Sephardic & Araucanian strands
but thank this native breeze & inclement sun
for their lesser glow they lend her still
brings back that trembling all over again
when on that day she answered *sí* I will

María's Radio

keeps her company & up to date
entertains her as she cooks & bakes
marathons in advance of weekly meals
each delicious dish will nourish & fill
the curried chicken over a bed of rice
Texmati or jasmine with an onion to slice
but first to skin debone & boil to a froth
to make the base for a tasty natural broth
for homemade soups of her vegetable mix
or of spinach alone so healthful & iron rich

her favorites the local Scot announcer-singer
Ed Miller on "Folkways" & Garrison Keillor's
"Prairie Home Companion" Terry Gross too
with knowns & unknowns she will interview
on "Fresh Air" & "Car Talk"'s philosophical
grease-monkey brothers who at every call
yuk it up as they dispense advice on muf-
fler ignition switch hydraulic lift along with love
together on NPR with "All Things Considered"
whiling away the only hours ever hear her dread
those spent starching & pressing blouses & shirts
will catch but bits & pieces yet it always irks
on just passing through to the "reading room"
where only jazz & classical would ever presume
resent not so much that pathetic Scotch-Gaelic whine
but rather Paul Ray's program of "Twine

Time" worse than Keillor's satirical lives of cowboys
horse-backed megabites in woe-begone voice
for it's Ray returns to mind her teenage years
*Sixteen Candles The Great Pretender Tears
on My Pillow Twilight Time* or *Party Doll*
when on slow numbers she will still recall
how Jaime invited her a great dancer a bigger tease

since his parents permitted no Gentile steadies
see her rocking in his arms around the clock
to *Itsy Bitsy Teenie Weenie Yellow Polka Dot
Bikini It's My Party Little Darling Only You*
till the green-eyed beast again breaks through
almost prefer at seventeen she had become
as she vowed she would a noiseless nun
no longer to judge a date by socks he wore
how well he could clutch or in soccer score

though not there in those days only later met
she already twenty-two & knew she was get-
ting a gringo stepped on toes & couldn't sing
couldn't stand his own forebears' Highland fling
a Texan given to the darkest of Irish moods
not half so smart nor clever as all those Jews
she's ever admired & yet will share the shows
that I may learn through her of trumpet solos
by Marvin "Hannibal" Peterson of Smithville
then ride in our son's Fairmont cherry mobile
to San Antone & hear with him that live quartet
perform with the city orchestra *African Portraits*
will insist that I hurry out of the gloom & listen
to Billy Taylor analyze on "Morning Edition"
Strayhorn's *Lush Life* with its amazing changes
such progressive harmonies as she too arranges

María's Readings

run circles around my own
everything from *Walden* &
Mayordomo to endless articles
ferreted out on the Internet

before it was novels in French
but not anymore & except for
Little Women her favorite since a
teenager it's all non-fiction now

always she reads a bit each night
to help her fall asleep her head
nodding & then jerking back up
as once more she tries to finish

the same sentence then gives
it up after her book drops off
the side of the bed & has lost
her page & the bookmark too

the best part's when she reads to
me a paragraph she always loves
from Mabel Dodge Lujan's *Winter
in Taos* of Tony the Indian who

showed her his enchanted land
where to find an antique trunk
works I would not have thought
to look into like *Turn Left at the

Sleeping Dog* learning through her
how garlic is grown & of the Old
Lyme home of Florence Griswold
rented to American impressionists

with their Connecticut scenes of
painted trees sails on the clouded
sea by Willard Metcalf collector of
bird nests & colored speckled eggs

just such delicate things on earth
subjects of her secondhand books
friends she lives with on intimate
terms caressing not caring if she

bends their backs even wets them
in her bath as juice from orange
apple or pear runs down her chin
the unread poet can't wait to kiss

María's Reality

every day she faces it squarely
not one to seek the easy way out
but lives with mosquitoes & geckos
little known to her in her native land

when doctors diagnosed the cancer
she reviewed her life without regret
if ending then saw it filled with love
her own for others & theirs for her

though tired of cooking healthy meals
she fixes vegan dishes her diet requires
does without sugar eggs milk cheese &
meat—doesn't miss them just broiled fish

believes the hoped-for we didn't receive
proves oftenest to have been for the best
not passive nor complacent nor indecisive
is ready & willing to accept & take the test

blooms & flourishes as her pretty plumbago
even in this Texas summer's sweltering heat
although unlike that flower she's never blue
yet does prefer overcast to this blinding light

her dreams never unreal but take the form
of a simple desire to visit Taos in autumn
see her own grown children both succeed
her grandchildren turn out as happy as she

whether it's waking or sleeping or speaking
English or her Chilean Spanish even hearing
her on the phone tell her sister I never listen
to a word she says it's the daily dose I need

María's Redecoration

comes twice a year
when with spring &
fall she changes to

seasonal shades as do
skies grass & leaves
repaints the shelves &

replaces light-green plates or
blue-on-white with the yellow
autumnal set & then

rearranges furniture in the
living room & washes
starches irons & fits

homemade covers on garage-sale
finds her sofa couch
& cheap love seat

takes down & alternates
framed prints & exhibit
posters with mostly Santa

Fe & Taos themes
her impressionist Connecticut scenes
or her favorite Matisse

of a young woman
seated reading a book
on a tripod table

substitutes a displayed copy
of Thoreau's *Maine Woods*'
river trips for his

Wild Fruits moving antique
crocks from above the
pantry to cabinet tops

bringing back sailboats dry-docked
in closet or garage
to launch them on

the mantel again its
fireplace rarely used in
this Texas weather removed

when her keen nose
detected the reek of
rat droppings in nests

of its pink fluffy
insulation for must have
every six months a

different look to keep
mind & eyesight fresh
while I a creature

of habit complain but
then on giving in
lift cart & resort

to the brutish force
she's ever against although
she will allow it

as a necessary helpful
ill & in the
end I must admit

such exertion does renew
the spirit but mostly
the getting to see

her creative touch with
the old décor is
all it takes to

learn change is better
than same except for
this year-round loving her

María's Saint

is none she
depends upon to
intercede & answer

any fervent prayer
not being one
to pray nor

even to believe
angels ever hitched
San Isidro's oxen

& plowed the
field for him
though what goes

on inside her
pretty little head
as on that

'40s radio show
only the Shadow
knows can just

be certain she
loves his picture
as farmer gardener

& bringer of
rain will end
the drought &

ensure the harvest
his bearded booted
haloed likeness pasted

onto a piece
of tin with
flowers & stars

& decorative patterns
hammered around its
printed paper another

of tin on
the bedroom wall
& he's also

on a postcard
purchased from the
Santa Fe Museum

of Spanish Colonial
Art now rests
upon her bookshelf

all remind what
a saint she's
been to put

up with my
poems she says
have exploited her

Maria's Set Piece

there are those who visit the sea
to add to a gathering of mollusks
to find what's endured unbroken
at journey's end from underneath
some perfect shape has escaped
the battering from wind & wave

while here on the beach she's stretched herself
to tan to a peach her Chilean skin
her lips taking on a more kissable shade
eyes sparkling brownish-red forehead agleam
the salty smell of her coffee-colored hair
blending richly with her delicious deepening limbs

appetites running rampant as she bathes unawares
I leave her alone with her lover-sun
drift away for collecting a line or two
for a predictable vacation verse
though know the sea is the others' type
with its long-celebrated calms & swells

too like the ups & downs of my younger days
too removed from the daily toils & trials
no tempests since the quotidian but drips
with only the sink's rusty spot to show
& on a smaller scale than its endless tossings
high & low tides so clearly marked

yet in facing the ocean must now own up
to the pull of its timeless & magical pulse
its winding conch & irresistible reefs
(do these refer to the sea or her?)
sand dollars drying at the edge
of a booming spendthrift surf

etched with five-petal blossoms
done as if in India ink
grown truer than a machine could ever stitch
the orange-blue bits of lobster claws
the tracery of lines woven by warp & woof
the uneven crisscrossing of their angled coming

deposits of large reduced to small
on a wordless shore punctuated by sand-crab holes
not unlike the distant registered vision
of an artist's ordered rippled rendering
held speechless until it arrives
to burst on the flood of a silent tongue

the sea is circled and sways
peacefully upon its plantlike stem

and sinister designs of the foam

then recognize & acknowledge the collection made
of Williams' tremulous flower / of a translation tried
of Neruda's subtle eye & ear / though more at home
among time-bound artifacts of machinery & men
& feel how out of place foreign footprints appear
tracking up a delicate patchwork of undertow & tide

yet find such patterns & signs
now call for intrusive steps
in need of a poet's lingual touch
for linking of starfish to cities & skies
glittering streetlights & constellations
as relations on earth & in outer space

for floating undulating fields of corn & maize
for the garden of the sea to feed upon

more than fins or scales or a breakable shell
for casting a spell like a shrimper's net
over the shoal of leaping image & word
& caressing her with rays of this comparison-love

María's Sewing Machine

is heavy enough
to have carried it
as far as she

would have given
most men a hernia
for certain me

she making it through
Santiago & Lima
on then to Miami

where at customs
on purpose
she chose

a Spanish-speaking
official with his
neck encased in foam

couldn't bend
to inspect her bulg-
ing luggage con-

tained her treadle
her cast-iron heritage
with its top of warped

& cracking wood
not to be sold to
the highest bidder

wouldn't trade it in
for the latest Singer
with fancy attachments

tied to this
by all her blood
her youth & childhood

am to her
as bobbin
to thread

together
come what may
will sing her

through every age
who can alter
any cloth

hem or reupholster
slipcover
couch or chair

& with her
sense of humor
leaves me in

stitches of love

María's Sleep

is neither easy nor ever enough
since childhood she will attest
to having been deprived of
its refreshing renewing rest

if she can the sounds she makes
seem conversations carried on
in none of her three languages
nor any I have slightly known

in dreams she may remember
loved ones in her native home
Carlos Muñoz who called her
"Gnomito" his little gnome

he a friend who died too young
an avid listener to Wagner's
Tannhäuser & *Götterdämmerung*
Ortega y Gasset his philosopher

at times she'll scream with fright
from a nightmare ghoul or snake
when then I will hold her tight
until she is safely wide-awake

if she cannot recall her own
her sister's she never forgets
of a cat's mouth would open
to reveal its nightly threats

to eat or swallow her whole
until she told it to go ahead
& so it did but lo & behold
when she felt herself inside

found its stomach nice & warm
& though it came once more
she no longer feared any harm
having already faced its horror

of La Chimba she surely dreams
with Aguirre in his rubber boots
her mother's father on irrigating
caring for his vegetable shoots

of boy cousins smoked in the barn
who resented her tattling on them
but if she hadn't raised the alarm
they might have burned it down

of playing in the park in Curicó
a southern town of Jofré cousins
had fun with them at the Óvalo
those of her father Zoro's kin

there in bed his dad lay dying
whom only then she ever saw
his wife Clara so loving & kind
to her adoring daughter-in-law

more even than Gala's own mother
Rita who found her granddaughter
insolent & worst of all a whistler
but her dreams not likely of her

in mine she is sleeping with me
as still she is after all these years
& yet at dawn I can never believe
asleep or awake she is lying near

María's Smile

has remained unchanged with
age the artless curves
of her winsome lips
two front teeth first

glimpsed in Santiago's Institute
at its check-out desk
as she stamped due
dates filled patron requests

happy in her work
searching file & record
ever ready to serve
but ID card required

can recognize it anywhere
in profile years before
standing on rubble near
mines in El Salvador

her shoed left foot
tiptoed & her face
with its ingenuous look
turned from desert waste

to the camera lens
scarf covering her hair
knotted beneath her chin
homemade skirt & sweater

at sixteen captured in
copper country by Saul
a sweetheart from then
grateful to that rival

Dave Oliphant

for his earlier lust
inscribed on this picture
his "She at Dusk"
"Ella en un Atardecer"

after our wedding giving
birth & writing kin
desperately missed on living
in places always alien

on a teacher's pathetic
pay then returned together
to visit Arica's Pacific
coast with behind her

banana leaves & waves
she in yellow sweatshirt
with red corn-kernels necklace
so beautiful it hurt

her hairline straight between
dark strands combed apart
pulled back by ribbon
& rubber band start

these thoughts of how
her mature dignified style
she insists on now
has replaced that idyll

refuses to play her
younger self to dress
as if a teenager
then gaze at this

of a second grandchild
held in her arms
here too her smile
is just as warm

tender open if anything
still brighter no gray
untinted hair no wrinkling
taking its radiance away

María's Souvenir

    at the Ely market
    she found & bought
    cane poles too short
    too thin for fishing

    carried them onto the plane
    crossed with them where the
    Titanic sank would use them
    to prop up in the yard at home

    her flowers & plants
    not for any kind of sport
    only once a rabid soccer fan
    until she caught herself

    yelling & screaming
    out of control
    from the vendor's stand
    could view the Cathedral

    spared by Cromwell
    who lived next door
    on Etheldreda's dowry isle
    named for the eels before

    Dutchmen drained its fens
    its famed Lantern Tower with
    its octagon-shaped arch-
    lined hall-like nave

    its angels red & green
    hovering so high
    could hardly be seen
    flying buttresses

impressive as those in Spain
less decorative though
while far below
bishops lie at rest

posed with hands on chests
creatures at their feet
carved or sculpted
meaning God knows what

names in the chapel
like Allgood & Piggott
the first recalls in Altus
Ricky that boyhood friend

a doctor now while the other
an actor in *Jewel in the Crown*
played on *Masterpiece Theatre*
another unsavory role

such history the catch
though nothing she intended
her slender stakes
offering more to her

than civil or religious wars
royal wedding gifts
naves angels bishops
niches to her of little worth

those even less than slimy
ravenous elongated fishes
no luxury liner or raj competing
with her hollow jointed sticks

María's Squirrels

visit the bird feeders
whenever they feel the
need & over her
passionate protests take their

flying leaps even in
spite of chicken wire
nailed to grape-arbor beams
stick their perfect landings

on the red-metal roof
then claw out sunflower
seeds cling by one
paw reach with another

so infuriating to her
with their lack of
any sense of what
is right & proper

ugly little rats with
bushy tails are all
they are to her
who drive away her

blue jays her brightly-colored
cardinal males & brown-toned
females in loving pairs
even to tell her

they too must eat
it makes no difference
they she only declares
must learn their place

where that is she
never says but maybe
in pecan trees somewhere
else or digging into

pot plants in another's
yard so long as
they do not bury
their acorns in hers

unlike them I'm fortunate
to be allowed to
stay the same as
all her pampered birds

even when I have
misbehaved been inconsiderate as
grackles she hates &
these pesky irksome rodents

María's Tambourine Man

having to hear his harmonica & guitar & smart-
assed voice day-in & day-out's not the worst part
nor watching in the bedroom as the little space
shrinks while his shrine fills with bootleg base-
ment tapes books like *Song & Dance Man III*
his Brit tour on video re-releases any new CD

nor is it having to hear her *Rolling Stone* read
on a fan dumpster-diving to recover cigarette
butts for DNA to clone Dylan once he's done
digging in trash for any song draft he rejected
hear tell of more sightings on bobolinkdotnet
of countless biblical allusions in "Highway 61"

rather it's having about the house a superstar
whose lyrics she's gotten by heart *that* is far
worse or in conversation working in a phrase
of his when labored lines dedicated to praise
her every feature still remain unmemorized
unattended unlike his concerts so apprized

by millions swoon yelling his precious name
throwing any item hoping he'll only touch it
miraculously toss it back with his autograph
yet even with all his followers & all his fame
he hasn't heard or put together how much it
means her hummed "It Takes a Lot to Laugh"

how her "Slow Train Coming" can stop a cry
& her "Man Gave Names to All the Animals"
whistled can change the times turn the blues
or "Desolation Row" from lowdown to high
tried tuning him out swearing flat denials
was worth the trouble could accept Jews

in jazz & classical even in Tin Pan Alley
but not one aping folksy Woody Guthrie
every prejudice fallen on sweet deaf ears
she the best defender of a hopeless case
wins it with the zealous look on her face
by a music she has made of all these years

María's Tapestry

before her consent to my insistent plea

& contrary to the uniformed official who
at the swearing-in declared on February 2
this date you enter the US of A remember
is the most important in all of your life
meaning to say she had only married me
to escape the poverty of a dumb Spanish way

had never thought to leave her long thin land
but chose like the biblical Moabite Ruth
to take this people & place as her own
though that was prior to meeting the two
for once she heard the murder of words
in English & in her warm native tongue
knew our deep need for spray-net & rouge
& sweated from 100-degree heat in the shade

her picture of La Chimba now hangs on the wall
grew clearer in spite of the distance & days
from that Chilean valley of her summers & youth
till not to carry such a paradise about
cooped up alone in her homeless head
state to state & house to rented house
she began in Illinois to piece out & sew
with colored yarn & some remnants of cloth
worked on a burlap backing tacked to a rod
her grandfather's parcel near La Serena's seaport

its stream with flowers & white picket fence
its arbor with dusty grapes growing luscious
its garden with corn rows carrots & beets
its bees buzzing about their half-oval hive
its trees with her paisley patches for leaves
brown print mountains blue sheeting with birds

chicks pecking in grass the washing on lines
embroidered green vines all climbing the walls

made them to keep from doing the same
on having to move to South Carolina
to live in an apartment where a couple next door
spent half the nights cursing & crying
the husband slapping & pounding the wife
she weeping then flinging a book or a shoe
would thud where this crewelwork suspended
her memories had traveled far from their roots

further from an Eden I have tried to replace
to match with tarantulas horned frogs & snakes
nothing to blend with her worsted wool
cuttings from Darío's corduroys Elisa's playsuits
with such remnants she has graced this fallen earth
tempted to by a Texan's foul-weather love

María's Treatments

pain in her neck & all her joints
led her to the ancient Chinese art
of needles in ears & at vital points

& to try chiropractic for nerves
pinched by disks deteriorated in
her backbone's scoliotic curves

warped vertebras a leg slightly
shorter though such conditions
remain unseen & her beauty

ever unchanged ever her same
delicious self but then from
so many tender spots became

an untouchable from her fear
my caresses might harm & I an outcast
not permitted to come too near

nor to stroke nor pet for only
her doctor allowed to massage
stretch bend & gently

twist her precious limbs
the acupuncturist to tune
& soothe her tendons

for if soaking her aching
connective tissue with
Epsom salt could bring

a bit of relief professional men
did more with fingers trained
to feel her bones & velvet skin

to rub or press as I'd sit outside
in their antiseptic waiting rooms
she on their office beds inside

pinned or manipulated to realign
so chi energy might flow again
up & down the beloved spine

María's Voices

a dozen at least have come to life
on her lips I've stopped with kisses
though never meant to hold them back

each of a stuffed or porcelain doll
or of the part Pekinese & border collie
her first pet who looked like a frog

so named him Sapo her Spanish for toad
later had more of a monkey's face
with his hair behind like bloomers

flared & swayed when he wagged his tail
dead from the side gate left unlatched
his ribcage crushed by a neighbor's cur

yet still he speaks around this house
in her high-pitched doggie voice
though fully grown at ten years old

when we dug his backyard grave
under the shade of a broad-leaved tree
where he played among the honeysuckle

till now her opening & closing of lips
is a sweetening of death let out too soon
his punctured lung made good as new

•••

only her Chilean family & friends
knew at the exchange of vows & rings
I had married a mother of bickering brats

never conceived how so many more
would appear besides our son & daughter
how fights between the two of them

could hardly hope to match
the insults yelled & the tantrums pitched
by cats & bears & fabric scraps

so proud of her on arriving home
just dying to show her off
to kinsfolk only knew Fort Worth

when all she cared to ask about
was where to buy a Winnie-the-Pooh
those so certain I had gotten a child

who swore I hadn't a lick of sense
needed a woman could straighten me out
not be strapped with some foreign gal

had yet to outgrow playing house

•••

in another language they're not the same
lost is the joy of her open vowels
of the eñes trills & double ells

this Texas mutter like mush in the mouth
the way she mimics how I mispronounce
even the name of my native state

the one sure place I feel at ease
in courting days she thought it referred
to the percent of income a citizen pays

then came to where no junta caused her to
unlike those chose to take refuge
in a hated land they still berate

where her babes would inherit my brazen tongue
that is Darío & Elisa certainly not Pooh
ever brags he is British anywho

& reminds how the Scots eat oats
while in England where he is from
they throw them out to cow & hog

his way of driving home another point
how he is of a higher race
of the same lineage as the Avon bard

when who pipes up but Paula Alessandri Rodríguez
ex-President's daughter or so she claims to be
descended from the Republic's "Lion of Chapa Chapa Chapa"

baby talk for Arturo Alessandri Palma
how spoiled can hear from her tone of voice
she & Pooh antagonists from the very start

"You were born in a department store
at the one near T.C.U."
"Shut up fatty who asked you?

gypsies left you on the backdoor stoop"
& back & forth they go in nasty kind
till Paula begs that I take her side

then says to Pooh "They paid too much for you
all your stuffing's falling out"
reminds how he was bought where I fitted shoes

at the Cox's over on Berry Street
sent later to the one at Lancaster & Ayers
to manage the floor two blocks from where

at that rented one-bedroom
the barbecue smell kept seeping through
cooked daily across at that corner stand

a food she still can't stomach
as the reek of its hickory smoke
brings back her morning sickness

is a memory she won't forgive
of the horned frog sat out front all day
trapped her indoors couldn't fetch a letter from home

of the tarantula ambled down the walk
when we'd go to let her stretch her legs
these she still recalls

& won't let it be forgotten
how her cloth world with its button eyes
of Paula & Winnie-the-Pooh

has never borne such frightfulness
nor will ever contain the pain
of a pregnancy endured in Cowtown

though never once has she regretted since
the mix of her Castilian with this hick accent
in a son's harmonious coming

alive red-haired & kicking

•••

besides Paula's rows with Pooh
who any chance he gets
will crack at her expense

jokes on how obese she is
poke fun at her fractured face
poor thing suffers even worse

at the young dialectical hands
of Juanito the Communist boy
whose suave announcer's voice

will report on & by the hour
his same predictable party line
"I say that on that glorious day

when the Revolution takes control
the first to go will surely be
parasites like you & your Alessandri

with your only worry night & day
if your hairdo's straight
or your make-up's on

who wait to have a nursemaid serve
your midday brunch in bed
but soon enough our time will come

& then the lot of you
Granny Gala & María too
will work & eat & dress the way

the People do"

in Chile after the mere mention of Granny

his speech would abruptly end
for Rita then would interrupt

grow livid as if he really lived
whose politics she wouldn't hear
yet loved him more than all the rest

had made his fine brown two-piece suit
the one he wore each time they fought
at breakfast & dinner or at four for tea

at any meal her only care
to pick at him then hide away
the desserts she'd never eat

but kept them in her room
They're mine she'd say Why not?
rolled her own & smoked them down

till the day she died at ninety-two
argued on between her puffs
disgusted by that socialist spiel

when Juanito in his juvenile pitch
would attack with his prodigy's wit
all declared his logic best

but knew of course was just María's
all thought her destined for the bar
would write such briefs

as could not be beat
predicted how she would rise
to the country's highest bench

yet believed not a word she had him say
sister mother & every relative laughed
but marked their ballots all far right

banged their empty pans in the women's march
to oust Allende's Marxist plan
& had Granny learned that man elected

though gone before that storied date
her dinner sweets green with mold
she would have died all over again

yet still can hear her scolding him
when he delivers his leftist speech
here in this capitalist kitchen

her cigarette licked & lighted up
her custard fresh with every phrase
saved even now from & for another day

...

many there are have never known
the one within only she can hear
those too of dolls have not survived

from childhood towns to north & south
from Ovalle where water is sacred scarce
& Temuco where dampness stays & stays

where Gala got the habit she never broke
of holding her napkin before the stove
even when they moved where rain & snow

fall mainly in the Andes rarely down below

in Santiago where we'd meet & wed
source of her many voices in dialogue

some lost forever others picked up here
where I'd take as true Paula's invented chatter
her transposed letters of naughty words

those no Spanish-speakers ever understood
outside this home such listeners all confused
& to parrot her language made me a fool

the kids as well misled by false phonetics
by much of Pooh's grammar so incorrect
& yet a teacher's role their Mom rejects

till now we none can quite be sure
if the diction of half we've heard
is of baby puppy or chicky talk

or a child's proletariat squawk
our tongues all twisted out of shape
by imitating phrases her own creates

but need them all
& cackle on catching another mistake
the fun she makes of "O how great

how smart you think you are"

•••

the one would hear above the rest
is day-in day-out just her own
that's the one for every season
right for every rhyme & reason

the one can make me shudder most
more than any shout or scream
in a blood-curdling horror film
is hers withheld exiled divorced

when in a pique I've sent it away
down to her dollies in Ovalle
to damp & mildew in Temuco
to that cozy home in Santiago

forensics silenced deep within
instruments capped with telling mutes
won't share or let them soothe
until I come back to my senses

but how prefer any among them all
when each is a part of who she is
as in these years she's been to the kids
playmate & mother rolled in one

to me my star of stage & screen
my keeper critic lover friend

María's Wool

never has she pulled any
over my eyes nor ever
indulged in idle dreams just

gathers skeins tinted apple green
from natre (an Araucana's voice)
fern   winter bark   shawl of

Eve & palqui leaves whose
odor isn't nice & yet
from them an ointment salves

insect bites & their color
lends a subtle shade to
yarn from Lipimávida two words

in the Mapudungun tongue *lipi*
feather & *mávida* mount name
that town whose Pacific waves

roll endlessly in on beaches
where after earthquake in 2010
tsunami wrecked their summer resorts

but to her the place
mostly means the home with
dogs ducklings & children at

play of the man dyed
the fiber & sold it
to her no tall tale

of rocky ledge's magic wings
take flight & carry youth
& maiden to safe escape

from those oppose their love
but soft warm balls have
granted to this distant room

a touch of her longed-for
aromatic land unlike that Mapuche
legend with its trickster lore

since never has she once
deceived yet she beguiled by
me begged until she'd leave

forsake her towering eucalyptus trees
her Andean snow & come
with me to this flat

all-but scrubby State not knowing
here she would live without
those sights & aromas still

so dear yet given up
for me & now each
day each year she's stayed

has knitted her pungent native
plants with this gladness &
remorse this gratitude & regret

María's Yards

her thumb is not so green as she would like
though wherever she is things grow & thrive
trees she planted still leaf out some bear fruit
the blue spruce in Hobbs an apple in Malta
& yet from a year at Voorhees one at UDLA
little more than anguish has for her survived

in New Mexico on Yeso the ground bone-dry
sandstorms blowing the top soil off & away
on the landlady's trellis would trim the roses
while awaiting the pangs of ineffectual labor
then induced to deliver the 7-lb. 10-oz. son
later tended petunias as the hearing went on
to determine if the father would be suspended
but mostly she would let that earth lie fallow
too afraid of setting foot on the red-ant bed
with its horned frog's eyes squirting blood

in Illinois on Orput a captive to ice & snow
November to April or on warm rainy days
stuck inside from a sidewalk rippled to life
as a mass of worms would slither & squirm
but there the daughter came gentler in birth
& there her seedlings would produce new shoots
tomatoes for gazpacho & okra's long furry spears
strange to farmer friends stopped by to admire
amazed by her cucumbers watermelon-sweet
deep green three months then brown & sere
lined early with frost soon coated & covered
buried beneath a white & windswept sheet

in South Carolina the apartment yard so small
her patch out back barely enough for the dog
he tied to one board of a shared wooden fence
each time she went there & set out his dish

he attacked by the unleashed bully next door
there the poor sandy soil lay barren in shade
any sunlight blocked out by a thicket of pine
a mat of reddish needles overlaid the ground
till it choked all growth except for the weeds
while over those woods hung a humid reek
with Spanish moss strung from rotting limbs
would spook her back in to water the pots
to wash & mist the schefflera's glossy leaves
against spider mites spun their lethal webs
as administrators embezzled minority funds
one murdered some indicted one served time
she trying to keep that hole healthy & green
closing the blinds on glares from faculty cars
parked at front doors with rusting screens
maintaining her home as a refuge within
for kids pet & spouse whose only job offer
had lured her into Voorhee's alligator swamp
with peanuts & collards the only crops

then a phone call from Mexico enabled escape
to a climate & language more nearly her own
where the open-air market welcomed her way
of haggling in the smoke of fried *chicharrón*
there finding words different for familiar fare
elote for corn whose name in her Chilean *choclo*
ejote for beans she knew rather as *porotos verdes*
got a big chicken when she asked for *repollo*
instead of a cabbage for the Mexican is *col*
women with braided hair & stubby bare feet
babes on backs wrapped in handmade shawls
piled their fruit & vegetables in neat pyramids
& all clamored to have her sample their wares
a woven sack in each hand weighing her down
would carry home on foot as much as she could

past a real pyramid New World's largest known
on the trail of tears from Tula & the fish manure
from the Tree of Birth to the Stone-man's fall
diaspora from mounds of myth-sized maize
to the site of four mountains crowned with snow
where the Conquistador spilled the natives' blood
& near it in the backyard of that faculty house
borrowed while a professor on leave in Oaxaca
she'd set out Swiss chard for adding to meals
the iron in its colorful leaf & succulent stalk
but first soaked in water with iodine drops
to protect weak systems from a strong amoeba
watered & trained her on-loan bougainvillea
greeted by bells & firecrackers midnight & dawn
till driven out by flames from enmity's sword
administrators raised against a syndicate strike

then to Austin with its cicadas' rattling whirr
to its soil soon depleted & its humidity high
& yet on Lazy Lane worked tirelessly again
picking from her plot her Kentucky wonders
for nutritious salads shared with whoever came
raising her family through her patience & taste
through the lessons & grades & the bills to pay
earning & learning in light of her nurturing rays
till the landlord notified he would sell his estate
when moved to Irma Drive with its higher rate
where afternoon sun burned her red dianthus
fought losing battles with mounding fire ants
then read in the newspaper of a buy-down plan
an affordable home where could design & plant
those xeriscapes pictured in her library books

& so in Cedar Park would start from scratch
setting out a mountain laurel an Arizona ash

grape vines to climb & a honeysuckle cape
with its long draping deep-orange blooms
trumpeting a tune to hummingbird & bee
with cosmos to shoot up as tall as the roof
our world in her as if named after those
though their flimsy stems in growing so thin
slumped if unsupported by her bamboo sticks
all the days of summer fall winter & spring
sustained by leaning on her quiet strength
her very presence a compost a humus of peat
held or let go as moisture retained or drained
at her whispers to marigolds in accented tones
each rooting deeper to endure a relentless heat
but if talking alone wouldn't bring them along
pinched their heads off so they'd blossom again
for little has flourished from just her words
even knowing better have failed to respond
& not a place have lived has ever come up
to her Chilean earth or the Monets she loves
no venomous vipers had menaced her there
no lilies or haystacks bear brushwork pain

here on Mimosa Pass would come to arrange
pebble paths rub leaves to her heart's content
& through her seedlings to inspire her three
to sniff the pungent sage's pineapple scent
savor rue oregano chervil lavender & mint
but only after we built her redwood frames
for elevating her sandy loam & keeping it in
hauled & spread bags of odoriferous mulch
dug up limestone boulders where beds to go
sank aromatic cedar posts & wetted cement
to erect an arbor for her champagnale vines
& her rustic lattice for the Old Rose to climb
sawed cedar stakes with their perfumed dust

a ritual readied nostrils for the culinary smells
from her sweet basil baking or boiling indoors
outdoors the fragrance of her chaste-vitex tree
transplanted from beside Granny's double pond
the scene of boyhood games of Tarzan & Jane

now pillowed together on the old four-poster
view pink New Dawn out the bedroom window
its pale subtle blooms a rerun of Granny's yard
shown as if before it had gone to wrack & ruin
yet daily she dreads that recurring nightmare
reappears as if the deadly striped caterpillar
comes to wrap itself in & feed on her leaves
or blue stars of borage extinguished in mud
or a poison ivy or oak on her lamb's-ear skin
have applied the cubes for their soothing cold
but still she has dreamed of that notice received
must abandon the homestead & rent once more
leave the mums & zinnias have fed & sprayed
blossoms beaks dipped in tongues have licked
rejoicing in her bright-hued throats in hot Julys
nectar stored against January & February sleet
rock-cleared caliche turned with fork & spade
for calendulas blue salvia hollyhocks & yarrow
for vincas portulacas four-o'clocks figs & pears
thyme germander lemon balm dittany of Crete
some do well in winter some in milder weather
a man & woman may in every month & season
as this uprooted other who's honored the native
has braved my arid summers with her santolina
made the best of indigenous wherever it's been
a perennial herself who has flowered each year
more than a garden guide to her tubers & buds
mate & mother who cultivates by her is & does

Acknowledgments

Cream City Review for first part of "María's Bath"

di-vêrsé-city for "María's Treatments"

Illya's Honey for "María's Smile"

The Langdon Review of the Arts in Texas for "María's Complaint" and "María's Hem"

Latitude 30° 18' for "María's Voices"

Lucille for "María's Tapestry"

New Letters for "María's Mandolin"

Red River Review for "María's Alstroemeria"

Roundup: An Anthology of Texas Poets From 1973 Until 1998 (Prickly Pear Press, 1999) for "María's Radio"

Sandhill Review for "María's Heart"

Seems for "María's Dresses," "María's Kieffer Pears," "María's Maine Coon Cat," "María's Meals," and "María's Sewing Machine"

Over the years, various of the María poems were printed in one or more of the following collections:

Lines & Mounds (Thorp Springs Press, 1976); *Footprints, 1961-1978* (Thorp Springs Press, 1978); *María's Poems* (Prickly Pear Press, 1987—winner of an Austin Book Award); *Backtracking* (Host Publications, 2004); *The Pilgrimage: Selected Poems 1962-2012* (Lamar University Press, 2013); and *The Cowtown Circle* (Alamo Bay Press, 2014; revised and expanded edition, 2016).

About the Photographs

- Page xi: María on the Pacific Coast. Arica, Chile, 1971.
- Page 40: María, Gala, and Cony. Chile, ca. 1959.
- Page 73: María and Dave at their wedding. Santiago, Chile, January 28, 1967.
- Page 74: María and Darío. Sycamore, Illinois, 1969.
- Page 75: María at home. Malta, Illinois, ca. 1972.
- Page 76: María, Darío, and Elisa. Malta, Illinois, 1974.
- Page 77: María on the Gulf Coast. Corpus Christi, Texas, ca. 1980.
- Page 143: María in the Atacama desert. El Salvador, Chile, ca. 1960.

About the Author

Born in 1939 in Fort Worth, Texas, **Dave Oliphant** taught and/or edited a scholarly journal at the University of Texas at Austin from 1976 to 2006. In 1974 he had begun his series of poems entitled "Memories of Texas Towns & Cities," which was published in 2000 by Host Publications. Writing in *The Texas Observer* of the *Memories* series, Michael King reported that the 140-page poem on Austin "takes its place ...as a long poem in a modernist mode which makes an enduring contribution to the literature of its place, time, and country. And that's a great deal for any city to be proud of." In 1975 Oliphant began his series entitled "María's Poems," which he completed in 2016, with all 55 of the poems included here in *María's Book*. A member of the Texas Institute of Letters, Oliphant won the TIL's 2011 Soeurette Diehl Fraser book translation award for his version of Chilean poet Nicanor Parra's *Discursos de sobremesa* (as *After-Dinner Declarations*), published by Host Publications. In 2016 Host issued a second, expanded edition of Oliphant's translation of a poetry collection by Enrique Lihn, *Figures of Speech*. In 2015 Wings Press of San Antonio published Oliphant's *Generations of Texas Poets*, a collection of his essays and reviews on Texas poetry, written over a 40-year period from 1973 to 2013. In 2014, Alamo Bay Press published Oliphant's collection of poems, *The Cowtown Circle*, with a revised and expanded edition in 2016.

www.ingramcontent.com/pod-product-compliance
Lightning Source LLC
Chambersburg PA
CBHW021439080526
44588CB00009B/598